D1402395

The Declaration of Independence and
JOHN ADAMS
OF MASSACHUSETTS

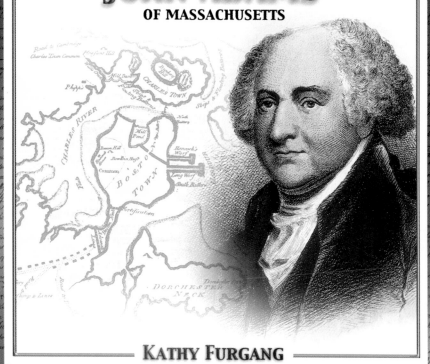

KATHY FURGANG

The Rosen Publishing Group's
PowerKids Press™
New York

J B
ADAMS 1/03 $13.95

For Susan

Published in 2002 by The Rosen Publishing Group, Inc.
29 East 21st Street, New York, NY 10010

First Edition

Book design: Maria E. Melendez
Project Editor: Emily Raabe

Photo credits: Cover and title page, Massachusetts map, written document and portrait of John Adams © North Wind Pictures; 000p. 4 (Portrait of President John Adams), p. 7 (Two Hemisphere World Map, 1626) © Bettmann/CORBIS; p. 8 (Procession in New York opposing the Stamp Act), p. 11 (Boston Massacre, 1770), p. 12 (American Revolution-Boston Tea Party), p. 15 (The fight at Concord Bridge, April 10, 1775), p. 16 (The Committee drafting the Declaration of Independence), p. 19 (The signatures of the Declaration of Independence), p. 20 (John Adams seated) © North Wind Pictures.

Furgang, Kathy
   The Decclarartion of Independence and John Adams of Massachusetts / Kathy Furgang.— 1st ed.
      p. cm. — (Framers of the Declaration of Independence)   Includes index.
ISBN 0-8239-5590-7
   1. Adams, John 1735–1826—Biography—Juvenile literature. 2. United States. Declaration of Independence—Signers—Biography—Juvenile literature. 3. Presidents—United States—Biography—Juvenile literature. 4. United States—Politics and government—To 1775—Juvenile literature.
   5. United States—Politics and government—1775–1783—Juvenile literature.
   6. Massachusetts—Politics and government—To 1775—Juvenile literature. 7. Massachusetts—Politics and government—1775–1826—Juvenile literature. [1. United States. Declation of Independence—Signers.
2. Adams, John, government—1735–1783.] I. Title
E221 .F935 2002
973.3′13—dc21   00-011919

Manufactured in the United States of America

CONTENTS

This is John Adams as a young man. John loved to read about law and government.

YOUNG JOHN ADAMS

John Adams, the second president of the United States, was born in Braintree, Massachusetts, on October 30, 1735. He was born before the United States was even a country! At that time, America was made up of **colonies** that were ruled by Britain.

John was born and raised on his family's farm in the colony of Massachusetts. When he was sixteen years old, he left home to go to Harvard College. After Harvard John became a lawyer and returned to Braintree to start a small law practice.

LIFE IN THE COLONIES

While John Adams was growing up, England made all the laws for the 13 American colonies. Life in the colonies was very different from life in England. The colonists were 3,000 miles (482.8 km) away from England. The colonists began to feel like they were not really British anymore. Soon they no longer wanted to follow England's rules. The colonists began to think that they should be able to find their own leaders. People like John Adams knew enough about law and government to govern the colonies without help from the British.

This is a mapmaker's version of the world in 1626. The American colonies (in yellow) and the country of Great Britain (in orange) were 3,000 miles (482.8 km) away from one another.

King George III of England quickly realized that the colonists were not going to pay the Stamp Tax. He took back the tax less than a year after it began. The colonists won that fight, but there were more battles with Britain to come.

THE STAMP ACT

In 1764, when John was 29 years old, he married a woman named Abigail Smith. The year after John's wedding to Abigail, King George III of England passed an unpopular law called the **Stamp Act**. The law forced colonists to buy a special British stamp every time they bought anything made out of paper. John wrote an argument against the Stamp Act. Many people agreed with John's argument. People in more than 40 other towns in Massachusetts wrote to newspapers and protested against the Stamp Act.

THE BOSTON MASSACRE

In 1768, John and his family moved to Boston, Massachusetts. On March 5, 1770, a group of colonists in Boston began to shout and to throw things at some British soldiers. The British soldiers fired their guns into the crowd, and five colonists were killed. This event was known as the Boston Massacre.

John believed that the eight British soldiers deserved a fair trial. He decided to defend them in court as their lawyer. John was so well respected in the colonies that other **patriots** supported his defense of the soldiers.

This picture of the Boston Massacre, showing the British soldiers calmly firing at innocent colonists, was meant to stir up other colonists and make them angry at the British. In reality, only two British soldiers were found guilty of any crimes.

The town of Boston refused to pay for the tea that was lost in the Boston Tea Party. To punish Boston, the British closed the port. No ships could bring food into Boston. Other towns in New England helped out by sending money, sheep, and other food to Boston.

THE BOSTON TEA PARTY

In 1773, King George placed a tax on all the tea sold in the colonies. The angry colonists decided that if the tea was taxed, then no one in the colonies would buy tea. When three British ships entered Boston Harbor carrying tea, the patriots of Boston would not allow the ships to be unloaded. John's cousin, Samuel Adams, got together a group of patriots. They dressed up as Indians and boarded the ships in the middle of the night. The patriots dumped 342 chests of tea into the harbor! This event became known as the Boston Tea Party.

WE MUST TAKE ACTION!

By 1775, things between the British and the Patriots became so tense that fighting broke out between them. On April 19, 1775, eight hundred British soldiers were marching to Concord, Massachusetts, to seize the gunpowder that the colonists had hidden there. Patriot soldiers were waiting for them in the town of Lexington, Massachusetts. The British soldiers and the patriots fought a battle in Lexington and another battle in Concord. The **American Revolution** had begun. The colonies were at war with England.

Patriot soldiers, shown here at the battle of Concord, were also known as "Minutemen," because they were ready to fight at any minute.

John was one of the five men chosen to write the document to be sent to King George.

JOHN SPEAKS HIS MIND

In May of 1775, colonial leaders met in Philadelphia, Pennsylvania. At the meeting, John suggested that an army be set up for the colonies. The Massachusetts Minutemen would be the first soldiers in the army. The group liked his idea. They chose George Washington to lead the American army.

The men at the meeting chose a group of five men to put together a **document** to send to King George III. This document would tell the king that the colonies no longer belonged to England.

THE DECLARATION OF INDEPENDENCE

Many people wanted John to write the important document in which the colonies declared their freedom. John thought that his friend, Thomas Jefferson of Virginia, should write the document. Thomas was a very good writer. He agreed to write the document. It was called the **Declaration of Independence**. The Declaration stated that in this new country, all people would be equal. Under the new government all of the people would have a right to life, liberty, and the pursuit of happiness.

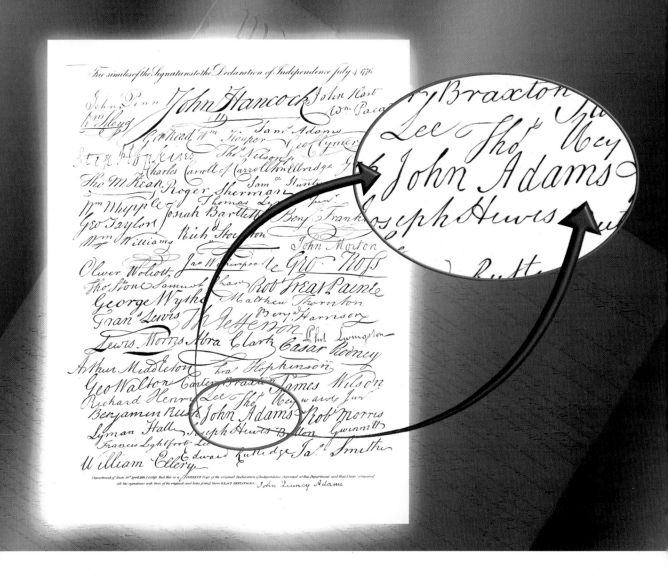

This is a photograph of signatures on the Declaration of Independence. John Adams's signature is circled with red ink. In a letter to his wife, John said that July would be celebrated for generations to come as a great festival with parades, bells and bonfires.

This is a portrait of John Adams when he was the vice president. George Washington and John Adams were re-elected to serve second terms as president and vice president in 1792.

A NEW AMERICA

The American Revolution ended in 1781. In 1783, John was chosen to travel to France as a foreign **diplomat** for America.

After the war, John was very busy helping to form the governments of the United States and Massachusetts. In 1789, John almost became the first president of the United States. General George Washington received the most votes, though. At that time, the second place winner in the presidential race became the vice president. John Adams became the first vice president of the United States.

AN AMERICAN PRESIDENT

In 1796, John did become the president. He was the second president of the United States. His old friend Thomas Jefferson was his vice president. After his four years as president, John moved back to his Massachusetts farm with his wife and family. Abigail died in 1818. She and John had been married for 53 years, and had five children together.

John Adams and Thomas Jefferson died on the same day. Amazingly, that day was July 4, 1826, the 50th anniversary of the signing of the Declaration of Independence.

GLOSSARY

American Revolution (am-ER-ih-kan rev-oh-LOO-shun) Battles that soldiers from the American colonies fought against England for freedom.

colonies (KOL-oh-nees) Places that are ruled by another country.

Declaration of Independence (dehk-larh-AY-shun OV in-dee-PEHN-dens) A document that states America's freedom from England's rule.

diplomat (dih-PLOH-maht) A representative of a country.

document (DOHK-yoo-ment) An official piece of writing.

patriots (pay-TREE-ohtz) Colonists who wanted freedom from England's rule.

Stamp Act (STAMP AKT) A colonial tax on all paper and things made from paper.

INDEX

A
American Revolution, 14, 21

B
Braintree, Massachusetts, 5

J
Jefferson, Thomas, 18

K
King George III, 9, 17

L
Lexington and Concord, 14

M
Massachusetts Minutemen, 17

P
patriots, 10

S
Smith, Abigail, 9, 22
Stamp Act, 9

W
Washington, George, 17, 21

WEB SITES

To learn more about John Adams and the Declaration of Independence, check out these Web sites:
www.pbs.org/ktca/liberty/chronicle/declaration.html
www.whitehouse.gov/WH/glimpse/presidents/html/ja2.html